The Mental Scars You Can Not See

Laura Gorman

Copyright © 2024
All Rights Reserved

TABLE OF CONTENTS

Dedication..4
Acknowledgement...5
About the Author...7
Introduction...9
Tomorrow Starts a New Day....................................11
The Years Between the Dash...................................13
The Demons Drowning...15
Drug Expiration Date..17
The Words I Never Got to Say.................................19
Sharon..21
Empty Space..23
A House Is Not a Home...25
Who Is in the Mirror...27
Comfort in the Written Word...................................29
I'm Fine..31
Phones in Heaven..33
Mam...35
Lose Yourself...37
The Bottle..39
Heaven Called Me Home...41
The Next Chapter..45
To Dad...47
Same Season..49
A Letter to Little Me..50
Your story..51

DEDICATION

This book is dedicated to all those who are suffering in silence, to those who have lost their lives to suicide and to the families of people who have lost loved ones too soon.

I hope this book shows people that things can get better. There is a light at the end of the dark tunnel that you may currently be in. To get there, you don't have to do the journey yourself. You just need to lean on those around you, even if it is a stranger. The thing with life is things are constantly changing, and we don't even see it. So, my message from this is don't make permanent decisions on temporary feelings.

Like problems we face in life, the storm will pass, too. Remember, it is the storms that are the hardest to weather, which are the ones where you will be most appreciative of the rainbow at the end. You have only got one life, and you will make mistakes. It's the lessons that you learn from those mistakes that are the most important.

If you are struggling with your mental health or the loss of a family/-friend, reach out. The hardest part of the conversation is starting it. You just need to take that first step. Sometimes, we all just need to see our problems from someone else's eyes.

ACKNOWLEDGEMENT

To Mam and Dad, thank you for always believing in me and pushing me to meet the best of my potential. Especially when I could not do it myself and needed support. No matter how many times I tried to rebel against your decisions, you always knew what was best for me and managed to keep me pushing towards my goals in life. You two have done more for me than anyone. I know how fortunate I am to have you both, and I am forever grateful.

To my siblings, Daniel, Ciaran and Ava, thank you for always being there. I know we sometimes fight and argue, but it's what has always brought us closer together, especially now we're a bit older. I know there are often times when we have not spoken in a while, but I want you to know no matter where any of us are in the world, I am only a phone call away.

To my amazing friends and colleagues. You guys have got me through so much over the last few years. There are often times when I need to offload my thoughts and emotions to you, and you are always there. Unfortunately, part of my job entails seeing some things that others could never even comprehend. I very quickly realized that although the vast population would not be able to understand, your own colleagues do. Things affect people in different ways. I personally have found being able to talk and have a laugh with those who understand the best way of dealing with your own thoughts. Sometimes, we just need a fresh set of eyes on a situation and to be able to view it from another perspective. Thank you for always being my sounding board, for getting me out of the house when I really needed it, and for showing me that there is actually an Irish pub in Northampton (who would have guessed). I know that no matter what I tell you, you don't judge me and will always have my back.

To my friends back home in Ireland. You are my day ones. You have seen me change from the quiet girl who left Ireland at the age of twenty-one to the person I am today. I know that no matter what happens, you lovely ladies will always be there for me. When I often doubt my ability, it is you ladies who restore my faith.

One friend, in particular, is the person who inspired some of my poems. After sitting down to have a coffee, we started speaking about mental health issues. We spoke about the effects the loss of a loved one can have on families and friends. This made me realize how, when we speak about people who have died from either suicide or dying of natural causes, how often do we spare a thought for those left behind?

When you have amazing family and friends in your corner, they are worth their weight in gold. Without all of your support, I would not be where I am today. So, all I can say is simply, Thank you.

ABOUT THE AUTHOR

Laura Gorman hails from the quaint and historic village of Ballinamuck, nestled in the heart of Ireland. At the age of twenty-one, fueled by a passion for service and an unwavering dedication to making a difference, Laura made the bold decision to relocate to Northampton, England. It was here that she started focusing on her career journey in the ambulance service, specifically with the esteemed East Midlands Ambulance Service.

Through her experiences on the front lines of emergency response, Laura's eyes were opened wide to the myriad struggles and complexities of the modern world. Her journey, marked by compassion, resilience, and a deep understanding of human connection, has inspired her to pen a collection of poignant poems. These verses encapsulate not only her personal experiences but also the trials faced by her friends, family, and colleagues in the demanding realm of emergency services.

Laura's writing is a testament to the strength found in vulnerability, the power of empathy, and the beauty of resilience in the face of adversity. Her words resonate with authenticity and offer solace to those navigating their own paths through life's challenges. In each poem, readers will discover a heartfelt narrative woven with compassion and insight, inviting them to reflect on the shared experiences that unite us all.

"If you can't fly then run, if you can't run then walk, if you can't walk then crawl, but whatever you do you have to keep moving forward."
- Martin Luther King Jr.

INTRODUCTION

This book is an accumulation of some of the poems that I have written throughout the years. Like most people, I have had my struggles and moments battling with my own mental health. For someone who hated writing in school, I have found writing things down in a poem to be my free therapy. More recently, though, I have realized the effects putting things down on paper can have on other people. If one person reads my poem and finds a bit of comfort in it, then I have achieved what this book was aimed to do. Hopefully, it can make you realize that you are not alone.

If you had broken your leg, people would notice and ask if you were ok. So, why is it, if our brain is broken people are still too afraid to ask or talk about it? Just because you can't see it on the outside does not mean it is not real. When you walk past someone you know, how often do we flippantly say, "How are you?" or "You alright?" as a greeting, but do we actually stop to listen for the reply, or do we keep walking and carry on with our day? You never know; these two simple questions could have been enough of a conversation to make that person talk, make them realize they are not alone, and maybe even prevent yet another life from being lost too soon. It's time to change the way we look at others and our own mental health and start the conversations that need to be had.

So, tell your family you love them and check in on that friend that you have not heard from in a while. You never know what tomorrow has in store. So, make the most of today. As Eleanor Roosevelt said, "Yesterday is history, tomorrow is a mystery. Today is a gift, that's why we call it 'The Present'."

Tomorrow Starts a New Day

As tomorrow starts a new day, without me by your side,
Know I tried my very best to fill your heart with pride.
Don't shed a tear for me, as my soul has finally been set free,
He told me it was my time to come home, and I could not disagree.

When you look out the window at the daffodils beginning to sprout,
Know my eternal love for you, should never be in doubt.
But he told me my time on earth was up, and heaven had a place,
Just know I'm looking down on you, with a smile upon my face.

As the seasons change, like new beginnings, I hope you think of me,
For a life, free from any suffering, was all that I could see.
Know that when I left you behind, broken, I did feel,
But I never wished for you, to endure my pain, it's now your time to heal.

As tomorrow starts a new day, without me by your side,
Know I'm still beside you on your journey and will always be your guide.
Promise me you won't shed a tear for the life I left behind,
As happiness and peace, I have finally been able to find.

The Years Between the Dash

The hand that used to lay on my shoulder,
The space around me now feels colder.
The shadow behind me doesn't appear,
The presence of you still feels near.

For some, the dash engraved reads much fewer,
But the words spoken for you couldn't be truer.
The two dates carved between, for you, my friend,
The memories of you stay with me until the end.

People sit around with laughter and tears,
Remembering all the memories over the years.
The time spent with you we would never change,
But for just another minute, my life I'd exchange.

So, I will remember you for your vibrant smile,
You were on this earth for just a short while.
You left a permanent mark that will never fade,
For some minutes longer, I wished you'd stayed.

The Demons Drowning

No one notices, no one cares,
No one sees when you run off scared.
The topic no one likes to discuss,
In case the world throws up a fuss.

In her bed, the safest place to be,
As in her head, she can't be set free.
Afraid of the silence, afraid of herself,
She lifts the blade from off the shelf.

All alone when no one sees,
The demon brings her to her knees.
Convinces her she'd be better off dead,
The scars a reminder of what's been said.

Leaving behind a world of pain,
She couldn't face the looks of shame.
It's too late now to take back your words,
What's been done and said can't be unheard.

As you go on with your life, you mustn't forget,
People's mental health is at a threat.
No one thinks it'll arrive at their door,
Until it's too late, and they're there no more.

Drug Expiration Date

The first day he decided to try you,
Suddenly, the world was split in two.
He thought the high would last forever,
"Just giving it a try," he wished he'd never.

All the horrors from his murky past,
Were suddenly before him, he never asked.
The substance was now the dictator of life,
He lost everything, including his kids and wife.

Now, sat in a doorway asking for loose change,
He wished the drug was never in his range.
The thing he took to try and escape his reality,
Was the premature reason for his mortality.

The Words I Never Got to Say

Today he woke up to start his day,
Through the crack of the window bay,
He could see the world already grey,
The trees rustling on the glass as they sway.

He leisurely peers over his left shoulder,
He visualizes a woman another day older,
He sluggishly rolls over so he can hold her,
And whispers the words he never often told her.

My darling wife so kind, tender and true,
It's not frequently enough that I tell you,
I know it's probably well overdue,
I want you to know how much I love you.

He puts his hand angelically upon her face,
He leans forward for a gentle embrace,
His eyes widen and heart begins to race,
His voice cracks as he shouts, "Wake up Grace."

He sits up and gives her an abrupt shake,
But still Grace lay there and did not wake,
He went pale and his chest began to ache,
It was on this day his world did break.

Sharon

You were my friend for many years,
This morning's news had me in tears.
I know we had not spoken in a while,
Now never again will I see your smile.

You were forever out going for a walk,
But always had time to stop and talk.
The friendliest person you could ever meet,
Now one less angel strolling our street.

There is now three kids without their mother,
The foreign exchange children are another.
One night out was where everything changed,
The date marked where your wings were gained.

Empty Space

You painted a smile upon your face,
You told me just needed some space,
Now, a dark empty shadow fills your place,
Your presence we can never replace.

I know that you struggled from day-to-day,
Didn't mean you had to up and go away,
I would have done anything to make you stay,
Now, it's your memory that I hold onto today.

The thoughts in your head never made clear,
I was here all along with a listening ear,
Your chair was warmed and ready with a beer,
But now an empty space at the table this year.

A House Is Not a Home

When your house is no longer home,
When you're away they decide to roam.
The person beside you, no longer your own,
In your head, you are already alone.

The white walls are filled with words and faces,
When you walk inside, your heart it races.
Your thoughts all jumbled and go astray,
You've mentally packed up and moved away.

The person beside you, now a stranger,
The realization hit, that your life was in danger.
You don't recognize the silhouette sat there,
Your emotions stolen as you look in despair.

It takes more to build a home than just a house,
Like it takes more than presence to be a spouse.
Even if you don't physically have a lot,
Make sure the right person is sat in your spot.

You will forever be sat in your house,
Wishing you could go home.

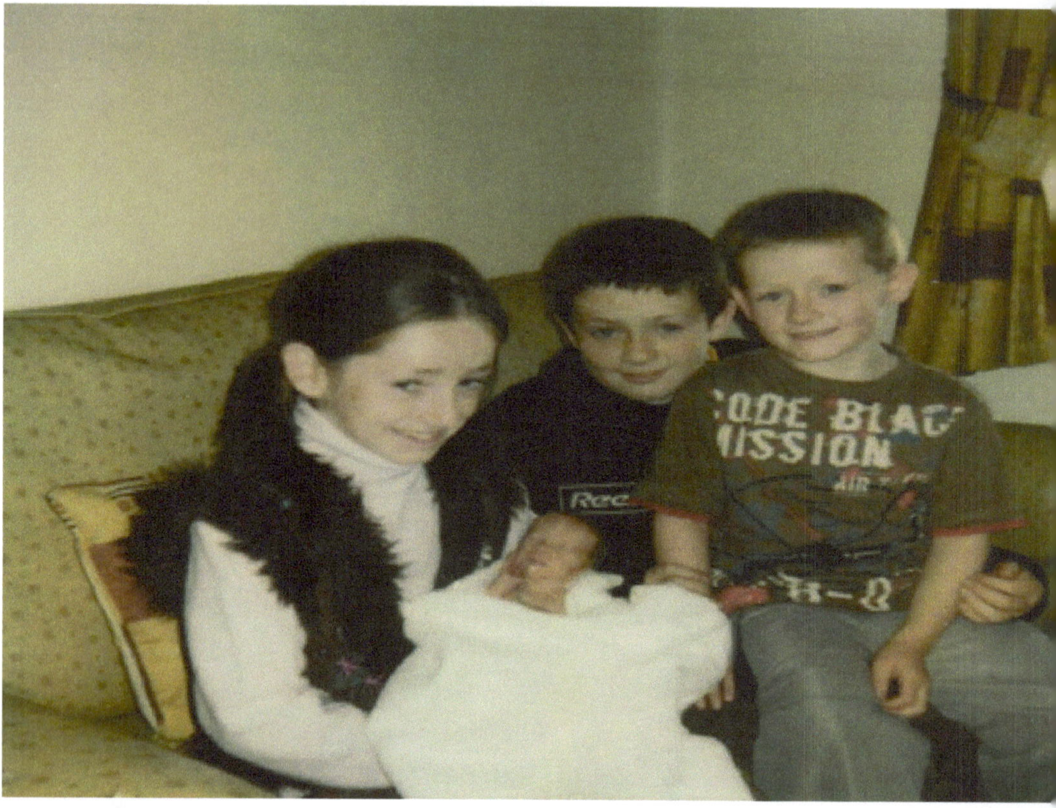

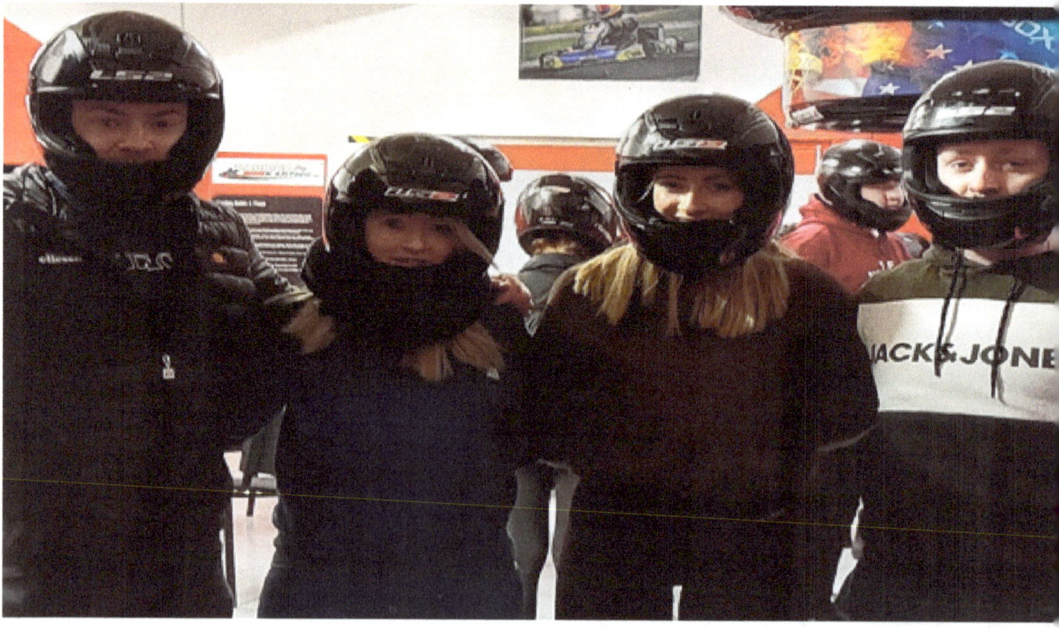

Who Is in the Mirror

When you look in the mirror,
What do you see?
Does your life seem clearer,
Or are you shadowed with scree.

When you look at your reflection,
What has not changed.
It's just a small section,
Many a look has been exchanged.

Many parts of you differ,
As the years quickly tick on,
When every joint gets stiffer.
To your eyes, I'm drawn.

They have seen some things,
Many others have not endured,
Like people growing their wings,
So, give them time to be cured.

Comfort in the Written Word

Close your eyes and hear the meaning,
Often many miss it with their own opinions,
Too busy with life, problems and screening,
Must keep in line and follow like minions.

No one around just the thoughts in your head,
Let the other voice guide your visions instead,
The wisdom and experience that's being said,
Let the wise make the decisions you dread.

When no one is there to guide your way,
Close your eyes and hear the words they say,
Knowledge is power when the lights grey,
The answers are in the music you play.

I'm Fine

Every day the words are spoken,
Get on with your day as if it's not there,
When deep inside your heart is broken,
Looking in the mirror, your soul is bare.

The darkness in his eyes increases,
A mere reflection of the man once stood,
His life is slowly falling to pieces,
"But men have to be as tough as wood."

Stand strong and stern without emotion,
The words you heard from a young age,
Don't let a tear fall and cause commotion,
Your mind is splintered and stuck in a cage.

"Depression doesn't touch a strong man,"
The external armor keeps it away,
Head-to-toe your eyes they scan,
Self critical thoughts begin to prey.

Is it not time to change the narrative,
Where "I'm fine" is no longer the answer,
A change in culture is imperative,
Before there's more male suicides than deaths by cancer.

Phones in Heaven

I wish heaven had a phone to call,
To make it back to you I would crawl,
What stands before me is a gloomy wall,
Without you beside me, I feel so small.

Please just come back to me now,
Without you I just don't know how,
A life deprived of you he should never allow,
To live every day to the fullest I did vow.

The big man has had you for long enough,
Life down here has only been rough,
Day-to-day tasks have just been tough,
Tell me you not being here is just a bluff.

I wish heaven had a phone to call,
When it's my time to hang up, I would stall,
Tell me I can still reach you, before I fall,
Inform the big man it's time to install.

Mam

If you could only see, what we see,
All of your worries, would run free,
The strongest woman, that we know,
Gets through anything, life does throw.

We know things haven't always been easy,
And without sounding overly cheesy,
We can't imagine a world without you here,
It will always remain our biggest fear.

We know things have sometimes been tough,
And we know we don't tell you often enough,
You have been our rock every single day,
Even when I packed up and moved away.

So Mam, what we're really trying to say,
Is we love you each and every day,
For everything you always do,
You will always be perfect, just as you.

Lose Yourself

You told me I could always trust you,
Now, instead of one face, there are two.
All my deepest secrets, that I shared,
To the world, you have now declared.

The person who used to lay in my bed,
Is now the name, that I do dread.
I'm so glad that you are now a stranger,
As the chances of losing myself, was in danger.

My trust in people is forever broken,
To you, I wish I had never spoken.
I'm now a shell of the person I used to be,
Never again shall there be a "We".

The Bottle

He wakes up at the crack of dawn,
Before he has even had a chance to yawn.
Attached to his right hand, is the bottle,
Now from there, his foot is on the throttle.

After about fifteen to twenty beers,
He's sat at the bar, full of tears.
He thinks the drink can drown his sorrow,
Not a thought spared for tomorrow.

He no longer knows a world without drink,
Only the sound of the bottles as they clink,
If only he knew, it was never too late,
He could start with tomorrow, to change his fate.

Heaven Called Me Home

Don't remember me for how I died,
My life and my death, you should divide.
Speak of me, just with admiration and pride,
For the laughs and memories, I did provide.

Don't speak of me, for how I had my last breath,
Or the way I chose to have my death.
Remember the songs, that we did play,
But just remember me, however you may.

Don't forget, when you get home and sit in my chair,
Know for you, I did love and care.
The adventures and memories we did share,
Just close your eyes and know I'm still there.

Don't remember me for how I died,
Know I'm still there, by your side.
To stay with you, know I tried,
But, another day with you, I was denied.

I'm Still Me

I'm still me, even if I don't recognise,
The person opposite me, looking into my eyes,
He introduces himself again, as he cries,
I don't understand, my mind is telling me lies.

Quicker than expected, my mind did fray,
All I really need to know, is that you will stay.
On the days my mind, can no longer recall,
Point me to our family pictures, upon the wall.

I feel alone and I am scared,
"I am your son," again you declared,
I'm sorry my mind, can't be repaired,
For the person I am now, you were not prepared.

I'm sorry if I don't recognize you tomorrow,
When you look at me, don't feel sorrow,
If I forget where I am, or my place,
Just give me more time and some space.

If I forget what I'm doing, please don't get mad,
If I forget why I'm here or what I had,
When you look at me, please don't feel sad,
My love, I'm sorry, if I think you're my dad.

I'm still me, even if I don't know,
Just take my hand, and guide me slow,
Dementia may have taken a big part of me,
But through your eyes, I hope, it's just me you see.

The Next Chapter

She tries to piece together, a heart she never broke,
Now being on her own again, the fire in her woke,
She'll say things didn't faze her and it is, what it is,
Now her friends gather round and sit, in the place that was once his.

Our story came to an end, so another could begin,
As no matter what I ever said, I would get under his skin,
As I piece together the parts of me, scattered all around,
At least I know, there's only one way up, when you've finally hit the ground.

As I begin my next chapter, I know some characters won't remain,
But the true ones will stick around and guide me through my pain.
When you choose the main figures who will stand by your side,
You'll know no matter what's thrown your way, your paths will never divide.

To Dad

The first man, who ever held my hand,
When I'm worried, I know you understand.
If I ever need help, you're only a call away,
"You need to learn" you would say.

As I left the family home, out to the big world,
If another hurt me, back to your arms I curled.
You taught me everything that I know,
But when I'm scared, to you, I can always go.

You have broken your body, so you could provide,
So, we could sit at home, warm by the fireside.
For the long hours, that you always do,
Our admiration for you, I wish you knew.

You taught me to drive, even through the tears,
Dad, I know I might often test your gears.
But You're the only man who never turned me away,
I know you are the man who will always stay.

Same Season

When they first met you, they knew, and the butterflies started to dance,
They would have kept moving, if you had only, just given them a chance.
Now they have cocooned themselves, for longer than before,
They don't understand why or what they're in this position for.

With you, they were ready for the world to be explored,
Now they lay in darkness and continued to be ignored.
Many big life events together, already they had dreamed,
But they were not in the same season, at the end it seemed.

They don't know if their wings, will ever fly once more,
They feel like, they won't be the same, as they were before.
They hope again, will come a person, who can keep them in the light,
As then they will know, they're the right one, and can again take flight.

A Letter to Little Me

Many people have doubted you, along the way,
I am glad you proved them wrong and decided to stay,
When you're sat in your room, full of pain and tears,
Just know, you will be where you belong, in a few years.

When people think you can't, continue to prove them wrong,
Show them your determination, because I know you're strong,
So, get up out of bed, and put a smile on your face,
As you have got many things to achieve and a career to chase.

I want you to know, there are still some tough times ahead,
Don't worry, you get through it, so there's nothing to dread,
To my younger self, I just need you to know,
You are going to get through anything, life does throw.

I want to say thank you for the struggles you bared,
As if it wasn't for you, I wouldn't have been prepared,
For the everyday challenges that are now tossed my way,
You have made me the person that I am today.

Your story

No one else can write your story,
Don't let someone else take all the glory.
The path you take is up to you,
Show them your individual point of view.

If you knew how the story was going to end,
Would you hit rewind or press amend?
Don't let someone else be your writer,
Show them that you are still a fighter.

If someone stole from you, is that not a crime,
So why are you letting them steal your time.
Your time and your peace they have already taken,
For their own benefit, don't be mistaken.

You are the person, who's holding the pen,
If you could, would you write the same again.
Sometimes you just need to hit pause,
Let's face it, we're all just clutching at straws.

Life is about creating who you really are,
Only look back, to see the memories this far.
When all seems lost, know you will find your way,
This is your story, and it will all be ok.

One Day at a Time

www.ingramcontent.com/pod-product-compliance
Lightning Source LLC
Chambersburg PA
CBHW040159100526
44590CB00001B/10